What Does God Think About Racism?

By Evangelist Louise Hamilton

Table of Contents

Acknowledgments

Anyone who has written a book knows this very well; It is an exhausting project, of course. It was certainly the Lord who inspired me to write this book.

I want to thank my Lord and Savior Jesus Christ for giving me the courage and the consistency to keep true to myself and just do it.

There's nothing quite as amazing as family and I am grateful for mine. I am a mother of five. I was blessed to have four sons and one daughter, one son deceased. Then three grandchildren and three great-grandchildren. They are all incredible, and I love them very dearly.

Most things that we accomplish in life, we don't accomplish alone; we need assistance from others. My special thanks to:

Mrs. Layne Smith

Mrs. Brenda Hayden

Dr Angela Sinkfield Gray

Cynthia Hughes

Bishop Martin Butler

You may contact the Author:

Evangelist Louise Hamilton

Post Office Box 210874

Normandy, Missouri 63121

FOREWORD

Bishop Martin J. Butler

RACISM or *"ETHNICISM"?*

Before we proceed to answer the question *"What Does God Think About Race"*, it would be prudent to bring some much-needed clarity to the word *"Race"* itself, and to how it is used today in our modern language. The word *race* is a word modified from its original meaning so as to construct a social hierarchy of humanity based upon the wide variety of physical features that vary from one person to another. From the perspective of those primarily responsible for the use of this purposefully *customized* word, it is from their vantage point and based on the physical features they possess which are used as the litmus test in determining who is superior and who is inferior, at least in their eyes.

Since God's Holy Word is what we will use as the point of reference to make our points and draw our conclusions on this subject, it is imperative that we understand that the Bible does not espouse ANY idea of racism whatsoever from the perspective in which society purports.

There are only four instances in the entirety of scripture where the word *race* is used, with each mention of the word speaking *only* to a running exercise and not to any of the issues that surround us today. See Psalm 19:5, Ecclesiastes 9:11, 1, Corinthians 9:24 and Hebrews 12:1.

If we are going to put this so-called issue of racism, in its proper context, we are compelled to view it through the eyes and language of Jesus himself. In Matthew 24:7 Jesus speaking on the social climate of the last days makes the statement *that "...nation shall rise against nation, and kingdom against kingdom"*. The word *nation* here comes from the Greek word *'ethnos'*, the same word we get from the modern English word *ethnicity*.

So our Lord was saying that in the last days, one *ethnic* group would rise up against another *ethnic* group and NOT one race against another race. To be even more specific, there is ONLY ONE RACE – the human family. We are all a part of the human race, but within the human race, there is a multiplicity of ethnicities. If we are ever to get an accurate sense of what society is experiencing, it is extremely important that we be more technical in the use of words and how they are sometimes modified to accommodate someone's nefarious agenda.

It would be more appropriate to label the social discontent in our society as *"Ethnicism"* and NOT racism. Every man and woman, boy and girl, by birth and genetics, is part of one ethnicity or another, but ALL are of one race.

But since the word racism has such a deeply entrenched foothold in the minds of men and the lexicons of the English language, along with many societies around the world, this book is written from the perspective using the word people are the most familiar with...*Racism*. However, it should be read and understood with consideration of the perspective that in reality there is only one race...the human race. More than 2000 years ago, Jesus gave an accurate glimpse into what we are encountering socially when He said, *"Nation shall rise against nation, or ethnos shall rise against ethnos"*.

In short, 'racism' is not a biblical principle established by the God of the Bible who created everything, but rather a false ideology

iv

thrust upon the minds of men by men in order to establish a social pecking order. This synthetically constructed hierarchy purports that the human family is on various rungs of a societal ladder depending on skin color, facial features, eye color, hair color and texture, geographical ancestry, etc.

Though it is all but impossible to rewire the thinking of the untold masses that have been made to buy into this pseudo narrative, it yet must be put on record that anybody who espouses the idea of "racism" as it has been commonly explained is complicit in the spreading of this societal propaganda that can be very easily debunked.

Louise Hamilton has done a stellar job pushing back against this horrible scourge. Using the Holy Scriptures to state her case, she brings to the conversation the mind of God. Our opinion on any matters of worth, especially this subject in particular, warrants the thinking of a Divine mind [God] to help us navigate the complexities of the subject.

Louise Hamilton, in her book *"What God Thinks About Racism"* makes us consider our stance on this tedious subject with a built-in question we all must ask ourselves, "Are we looking at our fellow man through the same lens through which God views His creation, or are we comfortable with the *status quo* of seeing men the way in which society sees him?

INTRODUCTION

I was inspired to write this book due to a churning passion regarding many of the things we see and hear in our present world. There are many today who have a complex of superiority to others because of some physical traits they may have been born with that are different from those who do not bear the same genetic features. We all are human beings, no matter what color you may be on the outside. We might be different shapes, sizes, heights, etc., but we all were made by God from the same material. The Bible says:

Psalms 100:3

"Know ye that the Lord he is God: it is he that hath made us, and not we ourselves; we are his people, and the sheep of his pasture."

Genesis 2:7

"And the Lord God formed man of the dust of the ground, breathed into his nostrils the breath of life; and man became a living soul."

Ecclesiastes 3:20

"All go unto one place; all are of the dust, and all turn to dust again."

We must know and believe that God exists; and that God is the Creator and Maker of all things and all people. When we look at the vast night sky filled with countless stars we can agree with Psalm 19:1

"The heavens declare the glory of God..."

We can look at a newborn baby and marvel at the miracle of birth, reflecting on the great design of God in every human person.

The evidence for the existence of our Eternal, all Powerful Creator is present in the world that surrounds us. Yet human beings have an amazing capacity for denying the undeniable...that God exists. Millions of people look at the same sky that we do and their own newborn children and still reject the existence of God.

The Bible says in Psalms 14:1,

"The fool has said in his heart, there is no God. They are corrupt, they have done abominable works, there is none that does good".

This thought is repeated in Psalm 53:1.

"The fool has said in his heart, there is no God. Corrupt are they and have done abominable iniquity: there is none that does good".

The explanation for such denial, of course, is not a lack of evidence provided by God but the fallen human nature which loves the darkness of sin and therefore refuses to come to the light of Christ. Some would say it is Science that caused man to be. Well, who made Science or Mother Nature or how did Mother Nature come about? Who made the sun, moon, stars, hills, mountains, rivers, oceans, seas, birds, insects, serpents, and all animals?

We are all the same, meaning we have the same fate in this life. Our flesh and blood, our hearts, liver, and kidneys are in our bodies to allow us to live and function. We all hurt. We all get sick at some point in time. We all must eat and sleep to live. We all must die at one time or another. No one lives on this earth forever because every human being is the same on the inside. Red blood, heart, kidneys, and liver are organs that keep all humans alive. We must have these organs to stay alive, no matter what color you are on the outside.

Many people do not want to hear what the Bible says about justice, fairness, evil, hate, or murder. Sometimes man is not punished on earth for these acts, but God is still going to judge them.

Ecclesiastes 12:14

"For God shall bring every work into judgment, with every secret thing, whether it be good or whether it be evil."

Remember, none of us as human beings can call the shots for our lives. I want to ask my readers two profoundly serious questions.

1) Why are we so racially divided?

2) Where are we so different other than our skin on the outside?

We all are born, live and die. We get sick, we eat, sleep and then we live for some years, then we die. Who can say I never have to be sick if I do not want to; or I never have to die if I do not want to. No matter what color you are on the outside, we cannot keep ourselves alive if we want to. We are all vulnerable.

Quite often we hear people say, "We want our country back." I ask, from whom?

Genesis 1:1

"In the beginning, God created the heaven and the earth,"

Psalm 24:1

"The earth is the Lord's and the fullness thereof; the world, and they that dwell therein."

No one is big enough, strong enough, and wise enough to take the world or the earth from the Lord. We all are under His control. Therefore, the world and the country belong to everyone-all human beings. God allows us to live on His earth for a while. We all, as humans, have a divine purpose for being on the earth. Many of us do not know our purpose and often do not want to know which is incredibly sad.

The late Dr. Miles Monroe said, "God created everything according to its intended purpose". Not every purpose is known to us because we have lost our understanding of God's original intent for us. Where purpose is not known abuse is inevitable, if you want to know the purpose of something, never ask the thing itself, ask the one who made it. We find our purpose in the mind of our maker. God's purpose is the key to our fulfillment.

The Bible told us to do this

Proverbs3:5-6

> *"Trust in the Lord with all thine heart; and lean not unto thine own understanding. In all thy way acknowledge him, and he shall direct thy paths."*

Also, in the New Testament

James 1:5

> *"If any of you lack wisdom, let him ask of God, that giveth to all men liberally, and upbraideth not; and it shall be given him."*

If you ask God for wisdom, He will give it to you liberally. He will not scold or criticize you for asking. Ask God to reveal to you what he made you for. Your purpose and plan that God has for your life, is what makes you happy and complete. It is neither the things you possess nor your fame or your popularity. Neither is it your money or material wealth. None of these cause you to feel fulfilled or happy. There are people who have all the fame, money, material wealth, and success but yet are the most miserable, and unhappy with a propensity to commit suicide.

There is a part of every human being that is not fulfilled until we seek our Maker to see if he is pleased with our lives. God is our creator and manufacturer, so the answer is in him.

In my lifetime, I have heard of so much good and so much evil that people have done in the world. The good outweighs the bad. I look at people as just people. Different colors on the outside, different sizes, different languages, and different cultures. But inside, we are all just flesh and blood. We come into this world for a little while and then we will leave. It is up to each individual how you are going to spend the time that God has given you on this earth.

Chapter 1

God's Love for the Human Race

Love is, without a doubt, the greatest subject in all of scripture. There is not a single book in the Bible where we cannot find the love of God displayed in some fashion or another.

God created humans in his own image.

Genesis 1:27

> *"So God created man in his own image, in the image of God created he him: male and female created he them."*

And God wanted to communicate and allow man to communicate with him, God allowed man to have dominion over much of his creation. He also wanted man to obey Him and be in a relationship with Him. We know according to Genesis 2:17 that because of disobedience, Adam and Eve ate from the tree of knowledge.

Genesis 2:17

> *"But of the tree of knowledge of good and evil, thou shall not eat of it for in the day that thou eat there of thou shall surely die."*

They died spiritually not naturally because later on they had children.

They could not have the relationship that God wanted to have with man. God deals with nations and Jews and the Gentiles and people and all individuals.

Deuteronomy 6:4-5

"Hear, O Israel: The LORD our God is one LORD: and thou shall love the LORD they God with all your heart, and with all they soul, and with all thy might."

Deuteronomy 7:7-8

"The LORD did not set his love upon you, nor choose you because ye were more in number than any people; for ye were the fewest of all people,"

v8:

"But because the LORD loved you, and because he would keep the oath which he had sworn unto your fathers, hath the LORD brought you out with a mighty hand, and redeemed you out of the house of bondmen, from the hand of Pharaoh king of Egypt."

God loves all people and He wants people to love Him.

Song of Solomon 8:6-7

"Set me as a seal upon thine heart, As a seal upon thine arm: For love is strong as death; Jealousy is cruel as the grave: The coals thereof are coals of fire, which has a most vehement flame."

v7:

"Many waters cannot quench love, Neither can the floods drown it: If a man would give all the substance of his house for love, It would utterly be contemned."

That's God's love for his people and the relationship between God and his people and by Christians serves as a picture of the relationship between Christ and the church. You will find all through the Bible that the Word is telling man to love the Lord.

2

Deuteronomy 10:12

"And now, Israel, what doth the LORD thy God require of thee, but to fear the LORD they God, to walk in all his ways and to love him, and to serve the LORD they God with all they heart and with all they soul,"

Psalm 91:14.

"Because he hath set his love upon me, therefore will I deliver him; I will set him on high because he hath known my name."

God is saying what he will do for those who have set their love upon him. God is love and He loves all mankind not the sin but the person.

Job 14:1

"Man that is born of a woman Is of a few days, and full of trouble."

Since we all have a few days on this earth, even if you live until you are 100 years old according to God's timing it's still a few days. God has given us choices as to how we spend our few days. He doesn't force anyone to obey him or turn to him, we must be willing.

Revelation 22:17

"And the spirit and the bride say, Come. And let him that heareth say, Come. And let him that is athirst come. And whosoever will, let him take the water of life freely."

Any can come, white or black, all human families.

Romans 2:11

"For there is no respect of persons with God."

3

2 Corinthians 3:5

"Not that we are sufficient of ourselves to think anything as of ourselves; but our sufficiency is of God.

God's Word is always the Ultimate and Final Answer.

The word of God is and has the ultimate answer for life here and after. The word is God's communication to man especially that which was given in Jesus Christ and in the scriptures.

Proverbs 30:5

"Every word of God is pure: He is a shield unto them that put their trust in him."

God's word can't change: The word of God is the final answer to life.

Psalm 119:89

"Forever, O Lord, thy word is settled in heaven."

The word allows one to see how to walk. The word has the answer for every problem we deal with on earth.

Psalm 119:1

"Thy word is a lamp unto my feet and a light unto my path."

The light of God's word is much like the example of the aisle light in a movie theater. There is a light on the stairs at your feet because generally, the theater is dark. The light will show you where to walk so you don't fall. That's what the word of God does in this life; it shows you how to walk. It lets you know the correct way or the wrong way to live and make decisions. The word of

God will guide us. We all should want to make good decisions in our lives and in our families. The word of God tells a man how to treat his wife and tells a wife how to treat her husband. It also tells parents how to treat their children and children how to honor their parents. The word of God tells us as humans how we are to interact with one another.

There are many scriptures telling us as human beings how to treat one another. I will just list two (2) scriptures.

Romans 12:10

"Be you kindly affectionate one to another with brotherly love; in honor preferring one another;"

Romans 13:10

"Love works no ill to his neighbor: therefore Love is the fulfilling of the law."

These scriptures tell us how to treat our neighbors. Our neighbors are not just the person next door, they can be anyone.

There is another scripture in the word of God if we consider His Word, we would have less hurtful things that happen in the world.

Romans 2:11

"...there is no respect of persons with God."

There Is No Respect Of Persons.

He said He will reward every person according to what he has done. Some people do good and some do evil. There is good and bad in every group of people.

My personal answer is that God is not against people's skin, but He is against the sin that people do. It is not our skin that sins, it is in our heart, our thinking, our mind, and our thoughts; then the body carries it out.

The Final Judgment Of God

At times we will try to judge our brothers and/or sisters. That is not good. We don't know what's in their heart, on their mind, or their thinking. Only God knows the inside of a person, we can only see the outside.

We were put here on earth for a purpose. Everyone and everything has a purpose for being here on earth. For example: a car was made for transportation; a chair was made to sit down in; a bed was made to sleep and/or rest in and food was made to eat. We must seek and ask our creator and maker what's our purpose. We should strive to help someone or some people in this life that we are given.

Not just to come into this life and eat and sleep and die. We must contribute something in this life.

Only what we do for God will last. The hereafter God knows what is done for him and what is not done for him.

Ecclesiastes 12:14

> *"For God shall bring every work into judgment, with every secret thing, whether it be good, or whether it be evil."*

That will be in the Final Judgment. God shall judge the work that you do for him whether you do it in secret or do it in the open, or whether good or bad. God shall judge it all.

But only what you do for Christ will last. If it's not for Christ then you or I are doing it for selfish purposes. The scripture tells us in Ecclesiastes. Ecclesiastes 9:10

"Whatsoever thy hand find to do, do it with thy might; for there is no work, nor device, nor knowledge, nor wisdom, in the grave, where you go."

When the scripture speaks it speaks to all human people.

God will judge all people. What did you do with his word when you heard it?

James 1:22

"But be ye doers of the word, and not hearers only, deceiving your own selves."

It's not enough to just hear or read the word of God; we must also be a doer of the word of God.

Everyone who was born on this earth will have to stand before the judgment seat. When we come before God he will deal with us in relation to how we followed his word. It doesn't matter whether young or old, rich or poor everyone must answer to God. How did you spend your days you had on this earth?

I want to ask a question here: Did you hate somebody's skin all your days on this earth or did you love your brother or sister? Do you love your neighbor as thyself? Do you help others or do you hurt them? These are the questions that only you can answer.

The Lord is our judge. He judges every one of their deeds whether they are good or bad. He also judges one's motives. Why did you do what you did?

7

Why are you displaying such hate toward someone? Do you do what you do because of Love or because of hate?

Some people have such a deep hate in their hearts that when they do evil to people they think they are doing right. All evil actions are motivated by hate.

God almighty can and will be the judge of all because <u>He is All-Knowing</u> (Luke 12:7). But even the very hairs of your head are all numbered.

God knows all of people's thoughts because he made all people of all colors and all sizes; He is the manufacturer of all human beings.

We all come from one blood. The first man; God made was Adam. (Genesis 2:7). Please read in the Bible where God also then made his wife Eve (Genesis 2:18, 21-23).

I am very passionate about the subject of race or racism because I know that God doesn't deal with people's race, it is just a human term.

God deals with every nation and tribe and with people's hearts.

1 Samuel 16:7

> *"But the Lord said unto Samuel, Look not on his countenance, or on the height of his stature; because I have refused him: for the Lord <u>see</u> not as man see; for <u>man looks on the outward appearance, but the Lord looks on the heart</u>."*

God wants our hearts.

Proverbs 23:26

> *"My son, give me thine <u>heart</u> and let thine eyes observe my ways."*

Proverbs 4:23

"Keep thy heart with all diligence; for out of it are the issues of life."

Everything begins in the heart whether it is hate, fear, murder, lies, love, or forgiveness.

People who have hate in their hearts transfer that hate to your heart. And sooner or later, you will do something evil. Evil will cause you to hurt or even murder. One must keep evil and hate out of their heart. Love and forgiveness are what we should keep in our hearts.

The Love of God – God Loves Everyone that He has Made!

The way God has addressed Race in the Bible. As I stated earlier, the Bible has the answer; the wisdom, knowledge, and information we need on any subject. God has the final say about any subject.

The book of Genesis is called by some the book of beginning. It is the book where all begins.

Genesis 1:27

"So God created man in his own image, in the image of God created he him; male and female created he them."

So, we see according to this scripture that God created man in his own image and not in the image of apes. God is not speaking of his body for God has not a body for God is a spirit (John 4:24).

The same God who made man made the women also. When He said in his image, it is speaking of the likeness to God that lies in the mental and moral features of man's character such as reason, personality, and will. This is where we get our capacity for communion with God. Only Jesus Christ is the expressed image of God's person as the Son of His Father, having the same nature as God. According to Genesis 2:7-8

"And the Lord God formed man of the dust of the ground and breathed into his nostrils the breath of life; and man became a living soul."

v8:

"And the Lord God planted a garden eastward in Eden; and there he put the man whom he had formed."

The first man his name was Adam.

Genesis 2:18

"And the Lord God said, it is not good that the man should be alone; (He said) I will make him a help meet for him."

Genesis 2:21-23

"And the Lord God caused a deep sleep to fall upon Adam, and he slept: and he took one of his ribs, and closed up the flesh instead thereof;"

v22:

"And the rib, which the Lord God had taken from man, made he a woman, and brought her unto the man."

v23:

"And Adam said, This is now bone of my bones, and flesh of my flesh: she shall be called Woman, because she was taken out of Man."

So, we see that according to the Bible, God is the Creator and the Manufacturer of Humans, Man and Woman, Male and Female. God is the maker and manufacturer. He has made man and woman according to what pleases Him.

We see from this scripture all humanity was created equal: equal means all humans are made from clay. Race and gender were created alike in quantity and rank according to the Bible. Psalm 139:14 the psalmist is praising God because God has made him.

Psalm 139:14

"I will praise thee; for I am fearfully and wonderfully made: Marvelous are thy works; and that my soul know right well."

The word fearfully means how carefully and skillfully God has made man. Our hearts that pump the blood, kidney, and digestive system have all been made very marvelously by God:

Every part of our body has a unique purpose. Our mouth was made to communicate, our eyes to see, our ears to hear, our nose to smell, our feet to walk and our hands to be useful.

Because of the fall of Adam and Eve (Genesis 3:17), the curse comes up on everyone and all the earth.

There were many birth defects. The whole earth was off the course God wanted it to be on. I just talked about how wonderfully man was made, but one thing we must keep in mind is how God made us by speaking to the clay dirt.

We were made from dirt and that is what we go back to when we die.

Genesis 3:19

"In the sweat of thy face shall thou eat bread, till thou return unto the ground; for out of it was thou taken: for dust thou are, and unto dust shall thou return."

Job 10:9

"Remember, I beseech thee, that thou hast made me as the clay;
And wilt thou bring me into dust again?"

Job remembered what he was made of and he knew when he died that's what he would go back to.

We all live in this world but for a few days. Job said:

Job 14:1

"Man that is born of a woman is of few days, and full of trouble."

Even if one lives until he or she is 100, it's still only a few days according to God's time clock.

According to the Bible, which is God's word, when we die we go back to dirt. We all live on this earth we all are going to have trouble, and none is trouble-free.

When God looks at mankind that he has made he looks at their hearts. God is not impressed with the outward appearance.

We as humans are impressed by good looks, riches, education, gifts, personality, or fame. When God selected a king for Israel he sent Samuel to Jesse's house and anointed him a king from Jesse's seven (7) sons.

1 Samuel 16:6-7

"And it came to pass, when they were come, that he looked on Eliab, and said, Surely the Lord's anointed is before him."

v7:

"But the Lord said unto Samuel, look not on his countenance, or on the height of his stature; because I have refused him: for the Lord see not as man sees; for man look on the outward appearance, but the Lord looks on the heart."

12

God looks at man differently than humans look at each other. We define people most times by outward things, but that's the only thing we can see is their outside.

God can see their heart and he knows everything there is to know about them.

Psalm 139: 1-4

"O Lord, thou hast searched me, and known me."

v2:

"Thou know my down sitting and mine uprising, thou understands my thought afar off."

v3:

"Thou compass my path and my lying down, and art acquainted with all my ways."

v4:

"For there is not a word in my tongue, but, lo, O Lord, thou know it altogether."

Just think, God knows all this about mankind and yet He Loves us. He loved us so much until He sent His Only Son to die for us.

John 3:16

"For God so loved the world, that he gave his only begotten Son, that whosoever believeth in him should not perish, but have everlasting life."

Romans 5:8 says God loved us while we were sinners. He doesn't love sin, but he loves the person and he places value on them.

So, how does God feel about all people? (He loves them) he wants to <u>save</u> them and take them to heaven with him.

2 Peter 3:

"The Lord is not slack concerning his promise, as some men count slackness; but is longsuffering to us-ward, not willing that any should perish, but that all should come to repentance."

From the scripture we see God has made all men. God loves all men, women, and children. All are precious in his sight. I will repeat again God hates sin; but loves the person. Only God alone can do that.

We as humans will hate people if anyone does us wrong, we don't want to be bothered. Many people will hate without a cause.

There are some Races of people that think they are superior to other Races. God has no respect of persons.

Philippians 2:5

"Let this mind be in you, which was also in Christ Jesus:"

We need the Holy Spirit to think like Jesus. So, if you don't like a certain race of people, you are not thinking like God. You're thinking wrong and God is surely not pleased with that.

The Word of God Tells Us in Romans 12:3,

"For I say, through the grace given unto me, to every man that is among you, not to think of himself more highly than he ought to think; but to think soberly, according as God hath dealt to every man the measure of faith."

From this scripture we see everything start from our thinking. It starts with our thinking we can renew our minds and think according to the word of God. The word of God has told us how to treat one another.

1 John 4:7-8

"Beloved, let us love one another: for love is of God; and everyone that love is born of God, and know God."

v8:

"He that loves not knows not God; for God is love."

God has commanded us to love one another. Red, yellow, black, and white we all must love. It is much easier when we have the power of the Holy Spirit.

Romans 5:5

"And hope makes not ashamed; because the love of God is shed abroad in our hearts by the Holy Ghost which is given unto us."

You may find in this book I have repeated myself many times. That is because we must know and never forget that God's Word is the Final Answer. The Bible says in Romans 13:8

"Owe no man anything but to love one another: for he that loves another hath fulfilled the law."

This scripture tells us that we are in debt to one another and that debt is to Love one another. What we owe our fellow man to love them.

It's not saying that we should make everyone your running buddy, you can't mix with everyone, but you can love them. If they are in need and you can help them, do so, that is showing love.

Chapter 2

Hate: A Very Strong Emotion

There are so many people today in our society that seriously hate others they don't even know. They may have never even met that person, but they just hate him or her because of the color of their skin. But your skin is not the real you, it is more so just an outward uniform that gives the world some idea of what ethnic group one belongs to. It's your heart, mind, your thinking, your character that make up the real person and no one knows your heart or your thoughts. God knows you inside out. It is He that tries the hearts of men.

Hate is a very strong emotion that brings out the most negative side of a person's character. It is ugly, repulsive, detestable, revolting, unpleasant, and is a downright unintelligent way to feel toward someone you do not know.

Throughout my life, I have observed many people who hate others they don't even know, and have never met. Though they don't know that person, they hate him or her anyway. Why? Because that person has a skin color that just happens to be of a darker hue than theirs.

We have a misplaced method whereby we judge others when we use skin color as the true test of one's character. Dr. King stated he wanted his children to live in a world where "they would not be judged by the color of their skin but by the content of their character". It is in a person's heart; one of the deepest components of his makeup where this character is found.

The heart is a place within a person's being that only God has access to and which He can only judge accurately. As stated in Psalm 139:1-4:

V1:

> *"O Lord, thou hast searched me, and known me."*

v2:

> *"Thou know my down sitting and mine uprising, thou understand my thought afar off."*

v3:

> *"Thou compasses my path and my lying down, and art acquainted with all my ways."*

v4:

> *"For there is not a word in my tongue, but, lo, O Lord, thou know it altogether."*

I have repeated many times we just can't leave God out of the scenario as we live life on this earth. He is all-knowing and sees you and me no matter where we go or what we do.

Hate is a very serious thing. God says in the Bible hate is not good for you and you don't function very well when you hate people.

Hate is an evil scourge on the human family. Do you want to keep hating? If one continues hating, it will fester into something unmanageable and monstrous. It is an emotion that the Bible has called *murder*. It is as close as one can go just short of committing the physical act of murder. Any person who is governed by this emotion has automatically forfeited any opportunity of eternal life. According to 1 John 3:15

"Whosoever hates his brother is a murderer: and that no murderer has eternal life abiding in him."

It is in your inner being where all your thinking and decision-making regarding love, hate, happiness, sadness, action, or reaction are made. It is *not* your skin on the outside that thinks or makes these decisions for your heart.

Since we are not responsible for our existence it is important to confer with the one who made us to help in guiding us how we should govern our hearts through these multiple emotions. Psalm 100:3 makes the statement:

"know you not that the LORD He is God, it is He that has made us and not we did not make ourselves; we are His people and the sheep of His pasture".

If we think we are self-made then we happen to fall into a state of illness then we should have the power to heal ourselves, telling sickness to "go away, come again another day". Again, when it comes to the place when we are dying, we should be so much in control that we can tell death "Go away, I am not ready to leave this world".

But of course, no mortal man has the power to reverse sickness or to change our reset appointments with the Grim Reaper. God ONLY has the power and authority to command sickness and death.

Therefore it is not reasonable, nor logical to hate someone whom God has made in his own image. For it is a direct offense to the Almighty when we dislike someone who was made in His image, but yet happens to have an outward appearance that is different from the one the same God gave to us.

If you happen to be a person who falls into this category, please ask yourself this question, "Why do I hate someone that God made, while at the same time claiming it is the same God who created me? What would make you more special than the person who doesn't look like you when it is the same God who made us all out of one blood? You have the choice to ask God what was His purpose in making people with a variety of skin colors. You may also while you are asking, ask Him which color is the most superior to the others; if there be such a thing.

If you are honest with yourself, you already know what He would say to you. For God has already spoken to us through His word. He perhaps would tell you as He made King Nebuchadnezzar understand in Daniel 4:35:

"All the inhabitants of the earth are reputed as nothing: and He does what He wills in the army of heaven and among the inhabitants of earth: and none can stay His hand, or say unto Him, What are you doing"?

Nebuchadnezzar was humbled by God because of his arrogance, driven from living in civil society to live among the wild beasts of the field. The Bible says he did eat grass like the oxen, his body wet with the dew of heaven till his hair resembled eagles' feathers, and his nails had grown long and uncut so much they looked like birds' claws.

It was pride that caused the fall of Nebuchadnezzar. God not only hated the pride Nebuchadnezzar exemplified, but He also hated it when it was shown in people who believe they are superior to others because they believe they have physical features that are more desirable, and which they falsely purport to be the standard by which all beauty is judged.

The scriptures are very clear about this prideful mindset. Proverbs 16:18 states,

19

"Pride goes before destruction and a haughty spirit before a fall".

Everyone who is deeply entrenched in this spirit of hateful pride is in for a great fall, either in the day in which he now lives or in the day when God shall judge the actions of all of His creation.

A better option would be for us to humble ourselves under the mighty hand of God. According to Proverbs 16:19,

"Better it is to be of an humble spirit with the lowly, than to divide the spoil with the proud".

One of the only times we are permitted to demonstrate this emotion is when it comes to the fear of the LORD. The fear of the LORD, according to Proverbs 8:13,

"is to hate evil: pride and arrogance and the evil way, and the forward mouth, do I hate."

Fear in this context has to do first with a reverence for God as being our Creator and Judge; a godly respect for the One who has all of our lives in His hand. We therefore are to hate what He hates and love the things He loves. We can hate the evil actions and words of a person without hating the person. Oftentimes this mindset is born out of a sense of pride and arrogance, entitlement, and a false idea of superiority. The Bible refutes this way of thinking by declaring,

"All flesh is as grass and the glory of man is as the flower of the field; the grass withers and the glory fades. But the word of the Lord endures forever."

This is how God in the bible looks at hate. It is a very serious thing with God, for God is Love, NOT HATE.

1 John 2:11

"Anyone who hates his brother is in darkness and walks in darkness, and does not know where he is going, because the darkness has blinded his eyes."

When we make every decision based primarily on the color of our skin as to whether or not we are going to treat someone with dignity and respect, we are already operating from a standpoint of being morally underdeveloped. That person who bases his or her choice of how they are going to treat someone on skin color is a very stunted-thinking individual.

You have made that decision based on skin color but the decision to love or hate came out of your heart. Jesus said "…out of the heart proceed evil thoughts, murders, adulteries, fornications, thefts, false witness and blasphemies. All of these conditions of the heart start with a thought to love or not to love.

Proverbs 4:23 encourages us to guard our hearts with all diligence.

"Keep thy heart with all diligence; for out of it are the issues of life."

One should not live life based solely on skin color. We must see ourselves through the lens of the Holy Scriptures, asking the questions, "Do I see people as the God who made them see them and do I judge people's worth according to what skin tone they have been given by God?" If so then there has to be some adjustment in our whole outlook on life. Seeking God and being in alignment with His word is the only thing that can help change a person from being a hater of people to being a lover of those who look totally different from the way we look.

Chapter 3

Love: The Antidote for Hate

God said: We owe, one another Love:

Romans 13:8-10

"Owe no man anything, but to love one another: for he that loveth another hath fulfilled the law."

What this scripture is saying, if you Love one another you won't need a commandment.

The 10 Commandments says:

v9

"For this, Thou shalt not commit adultery, Thou shalt not kill, Thou shalt not steal, Thou shalt not bear false witness, Thou shalt not covet; and if there be any other commandment, it is briefly comprehended in this saying, namely, Thou shalt love thy neighbour as thyself."

Because:

v10

"Love works no ill to his neighbor: therefore love is the fulfilling of the law."

What does the world need now, since we already have so much Hate all over the world? The answer is Love. So how, does one get this power to Love someone when you know that they don't Love you?

The Bible says:

Acts 1:8a

> *"But ye shall receive power, after that the Holy Ghost is come upon you;"*

Also in:

Romans 5:5

> *"Hope makes not ashamed; because the love of God is shed abroad in our hearts by the Holy Ghost which is given unto us."*

That is, if anyone wants his power, it comes through the Holy Spirit.

God doesn't force anyone to receive his power, one must want his power.

The Last Invitation:

Revelation 22:17

> *"And the Spirit and the bride say, Come. And let him that hears say, Come. And let him that is athirst come. And whosoever will, let him take the water of life freely."*

There are many times when God tells us to Love.

1 John 4:7-8

> *"Beloved, let us love one another: for love is of God; and everyone that love is born of God, and knows God."*

v8

> *"He that Love not knows not God; <u>for God is Love</u>."*

1 John 4:20-21

"If a man say, I love God, and hate his brother, he is a liar: for he that loves not his brother whom he hath seen, how can he love God whom he hath not seen?"

v21

"And this commandment have we from him, that he who loveth God love his brother also."

God has commanded us to Love our enemies. It will take God's power to obey that command.

Matthew 5:44

"But I say unto you, love your enemies, bless them that curse you, do good to them that hate you, and pray for them which despitefully use you, and persecute you;"

How can one Love a person when you know they are an enemy. God said in:

Proverbs 25: 21-22

"If thine enemy be hungry give him bread to eat; and if he be thirsty, give him water to drink;"

v22

"For thou shall heap coals of fire upon his head, and the <u>Lord shall reward</u> thee."

John 3:16

"For God so loved the world, that he gave his only begotten Son, that whosoever believeth in him should not perish, but have everlasting life."

God Loves the World, that is, the people who are in the World.

He doesn't Love the Sin but He Loves the Sinner.

He said in his words that He makes His sun rise on the evil and on the good and sends rain on the just and on the unjust.

For if ye love them which love you, what reward have ye? Do not even the pagans do this?

God tells us we have to allow the same mind to be in us that he has.

Philippians 2:5

"Let this mind be in you, which was also in Christ Jesus: "

We are the Most Like God When We are Loving! Because God is Love. Love is Truly the Antidote for Hate.

Chapter 4

How to Treat One Another

First, regarding the way we treat God's people: whatever is done to God's people, God considers it done unto Him.

Acts 9:1-5

"And Saul, yet breathing out threatening and slaughter against the disciples of the Lord, went unto the high priest,"

v3

"and as he journeyed, he came near Damascus: and suddenly there shined round about him a light from heaven;"

v4

"and he fell to the earth, and heard a voice saying unto him, Saul, Saul, why persecutest thou me?"

V5:

"And he said, who art thou, Lord? And the Lord said, I am Jesus whom thou persecutest: it is hard for thee to kick against the pricks."

Romans 12:16

"Be of the same mind one toward another. Mind not high things, but condescend to men of low estate. Be not wise in your own conceits."

Romans 12:18

"If it be possible, as much as lies in you, live peaceably with all men."

James 4:11-12.

"Speak not evil one of another, brethren. He that speaks evil of his brother, and judges his brother, speaks evil of the law, and judges the law: but if thou judge the law, thou are not a doer of the law, but a judge."

v12

"There is one lawgiver, who is able to save and to destroy: who are thou that judges another?"

Romans 12:10

"Be Kindly Affectionate one to another with brotherly love; in honor preferring one another;"

Philippians 2:3.

"Let nothing be done through strife or vainglory, but in lowliness of mind let each esteem other better than themselves."

Ephesians 5:2

"Submitting yourselves one to another in the fear of God."

Ephesians 4:32

"and be ye kind one to another, tenderhearted, forgiving one another, even as God for Christ's sake hath forgiven you."

It may be easy for us to treat our loved ones, our family, friends, and others with respect or even those we want to impress with respect.

But Jesus tells us to <u>Honor</u> all people and treat them all with <u>Respect</u>.

1 Peter 2:17.

> *"Honor all men. Love the brotherhood. Fear God. Honor the king."*

There is another scripture that tells us:

Romans 13:8

> *"<u>Owe</u> no man anything, but to love one another: for he that <u>loves</u> another hath fulfilled the law."*

Romans 13:9-10

> *"For this, Thou shalt not commit adultery, Thou shalt not kill, Thou shalt not commit adultery, Thou shalt not kill, Thou shalt not steal, Thou shalt not bear false witness, Thou shalt not covet; and if there be any other commandment, it is briefly comprehended in this saying, namely, Thou shalt love thy neighbour as thyself."*

v10

> *"Love worketh no ill to his neighbour: therefore love is the fulfilling of the law"*

What this scripture is saying to us is that if one would just Love, just sincerely Love and respect people, we won't need a law to force us to do right to people.

We owe people according to the word of the Lord.

Matthew 5:43-45

"Ye have heard that it hath been said, thou shalt love thy neighbor, and hat thine enemy."

v44

"But I say unto you, love your enemies, bless them that curse you, do good to them that hate you, and pray for them which despitefully us you, and persecute you;"

Jesus said:

v45b

"He makes his sun to rise on the evil and on the good, and sends rain on the just and on the unjust."

Jesus is good to people who don't even believe he exists.

Psalm 14:1

"The fool hath said in his heart, there is no God. They are corrupt, they have done abominable works, there is none that doeth good."

God is not destroying everyone that doesn't believe there is a God.

He is not killing people who don't believe He exists, instead He loves them.

Some people just don't believe that there is a God, but nonetheless, the word of God tells us we must be like Him.

Philippians 2:5

"Let this mind be in you, which was also in Christ Jesus:"

Chapter 5

The Heart of Man

The <u>heart</u> is the inner man, it is where everything starts.

Your thinking, your desire, it can be evil <u>thoughts</u> or good <u>thoughts</u>. Kind <u>thoughts</u> even loving <u>thoughts</u>.

Proverbs 4:23

> *"Keep thy <u>heart</u> with all diligence; for out of it are the issues of life."*

Jeremiah 17:9-10

> *"The <u>heart</u> is deceitful above all things, and desperately wicked: who can know it?"*

<u>None Knows the Heart; Only God</u>.

v10

> *"I the Lord search the <u>heart</u>, I try the reins, even to give every man according to his ways, and according to the fruit of his doings."*

Many of us look at a person and judge their appearance, their dress, their education, where they live, and what their job is.

1 Samuel 16:7

> *"But the Lord said unto Samuel, look not on his countenance, or on the height of his stature; because I have refused him: for the Lord sees not as man sees: for man looks on the outward appearance, but the Lord looks on the heart."*

It is not about our skin color or anything else but the <u>heart</u>. God chooses people from the <u>heart</u>.

There is good, bad, and ugly in every Race on the earth. God loves people but not sin. This scripture lets us know that:

Romans 3:23

"for all have sinned, and come short of the glory of God;"

But we have a way out:

Romans 5:19

"For as by one man's disobedience many were made sinners, so by the obedience of one shall many be made righteous."

I am going to repeat what I said about keeping thy heart.

Proverbs 4:23

"<u>Keep</u> thy <u>heart</u> with <u>all</u> diligence: for out of it are the issues of life."

(Decisions) thoughts of evil or it can be thoughts of good. What's in your heart?

Matthew 12:34

"for out of the abundance of the heart the mouth speaketh."

Matthew 15:19

"For out of the heart proceed evil thoughts, murders, adulteries, fornications, thefts, false witness, blasphemies:"

Psalm 94:11

"The Lord knows the thoughts of man, that they are vanity."

When people think of doing murders in their hearts, God knows about it, they may get away with it according to the law of the land. But they are still guilty before God because that is one of God's Commandments; Exodus 20:13

"Thou shall not kill (murder)."

A look into the mind of a man

Many of our problems and troubles in the world today are because we don't fear God. (reverence fear) respect.

Many don't believe in God or believe God made man. Their mind is like the Bible says:

Romans 1:28-30

"And even as they did not like to retain God in their knowledge, God gave them over to a reprobate mind, to do those things which are not convenient;"

Because God gave them over to a reprobate <u>mind,</u> they are subject to do anything.

v29

"being filled with all unrighteousness, fornication, wickedness, covetousness, maliciousness; full of envy, murder, debate, deceit, malignity; whisperers,"

v30

"backbiters, haters of God, despiteful, proud, boasters, inventors of evil things, disobedient to parents,"

God has another order, his word is the order, and the word of God is our guideline in this world.

32

When one doesn't embrace God's word the Bible is God's word. When one tries to define humans apart from God's word they miss it. God is the manufacturer of every human person according to the Bible all humans were made from dust (Genesis 2:7). Man was not made from apes, nor was made by scientists. The Bible says in:

Psalm 100:3.

"Know ye that the Lord he is God: It is he that hath made us, and not we ourselves;"

The scripture rules out all others. It is God that has made us and not another.

God made man the way he wanted to make man. If we had made ourselves, I am sure we would have made ourselves perfect. The prettiest, the richest, never get sick, never die, no problems and no troubles. God's word said in Job 14:1

"Man is born of a woman Is a few days, and full of trouble."

The Soul of Man:

Our human life on this earth is a temporal life, it is not forever. We will live here on Earth for a little while then we will be gone. Our body will return to the dust from whence it came.

Genesis 3:19

"in the sweat of thy face shall thou eat bread, till thou return unto the ground; for out of it was thou taken: for dust thou art, and unto dust shall thou return."

The soul is a distinct entity separate from the body. It is separable in existence from the body. The soul of a human being does not die. The body will but the soul will live forever it is eternal it has to spend eternity somewhere and since God has given man the power to make choices. We can make a choice to allow God to control our lives.

Ezekiel 18:4

> *"Behold all souls are mine; as the soul of the father, so also the soul of the son is mine: the soul that sins, it shall die."*

Every individual must give account for him or herself, all people on the earth.

Ezekiel 18:20

> *"The soul that sins, it shall die. The son shall not bear the iniquity of the father, neither shall the father bear the iniquity of the son: the righteousness of the righteous shall be upon him, and the wickedness of the wicked shall be upon him."*

Romans 2:11

> *"for there is no respect of persons with God."*

All human people are the same inside, God looks not at the outward appearance but he looks at the heart, mind, soul, and spirit of human beings. We can make a choice to do what the Bible tells us to do in (John 3:1- 8 and Acts 2:38). These are scriptures that will allow one to be born again. It is not a natural birth but it is a spirit birth.

Remember in (Genesis 3:3) when Adam and Eve disobeyed God, they put everyone in sin. According to:

Romans 5:12.

> *"Wherefore, as by one man sin entered into the world, and death by sin; and so death passed upon all men, for that all have sinned;"*

Genesis 3:20

> *"And Adam called his wife's name Eve; because she was the mother of all living"*

Everyone living person came out from Adam and Eve. All Races of people came from dust and will return to dust.

Genesis 3:19

> *"in the sweat of thy face shall thou eat bread, till thou return unto the ground; for out of it was thou taken: for dust thou art, and unto dust shall thou return."*

It continues to say this truth: All races of people must die at some time or another. Death doesn't have an age or Race. Kings die, queens die. Beautiful women and handsome men die. Rich or poor, no one gets a pass.

Job 14:1

> *"Man that is born of a woman Is of few days, and full of trouble."*

We all have trouble sometimes in our lives irrespective of who we might be. The spirit is the inner part of a person. It is God's agency. The spirit is the inward reality. The spirit is the characteristic of what's in humans.

1. *Center of emotions.*
2. *Source of passions.*
3. *Act of the will*
4. *The Richness of the Human Race*

I believe God gets the glory in that He made us different skin colors on the outside. However, on the inside blood is red in all His creation.

1.   *Heart*---One's inter-most character.

2.   *Mind*---Memory that thinks, wills, reasons, conscious mental events, culpabilities, and mental activity.

3.   *Your Thinking*--- Thoughts to have an opinion, to regard or consider.

4.   *Desire*---To express craving or covet a wish, a longing or appetite.

5.   *The Soul*---The spiritual principle embodies in humans, a person's total self. (This is the part of you that goes back to God. The body goes back to dust). When a person dies he is either buried in the ground or the body is cremated.

I will say again we all have the same fate. All people are the same on the inside. No one knows the heart but God. God knows what's in the mind.

God knows our thoughts before we think them:

Psalm 139:2

> *"Thou knows my downsitting and mine uprising, thou understand my thought afar off."*

He says all souls belong to him (Ezekiel 18:4) But the soul that sins shall die. You notice in this scripture the Lord says those that sin, that means those that keep doing wrong will die spiritually that's not a natural death.

There is an individual richness in all human beings:

Genesis 1:27

> *"So God created man in his own image, in the image of God created he him; male and female created he them."*

So, when we hate, we really hate people that God made in the image of Himself. People did not make themselves.

I want, when one reads this book to change their minds about hating someone; that is a waste of time since we only have a little time to be on this earth. Let's make the best of the time that we have on this earth by obeying God, caring for others, caring for ourselves, and living a good life.

Genesis 3:3

"But of the fruit of the tree which is in the midst of the garden God hath said, Ye shall not eat of it, neither shall ye touch it, <u>lest we die.</u>"

God was not saying they would naturally die, but they would die spirituality and they would be separated from God. Because of that one man's sin, <u>the whole human race was born in sin</u>.

Romans 5:19

For as by one man's disobedience many were made sinners, so by the obedience of one shall many be made righteous.

This verse speaks of Jesus making men righteous through the sacrifice of himself on Calvary's cross.

After Eve did eat the fruit that God told her husband Adam and her not to eat, they both ate and they were spiritually dead just as God had said. They were not naturally dead because they had children afterward.

That one disobedience threw the whole course off. This is the relationship that God wanted to have with man.

That one disobedience separated the whole human race from God such that everyone born thereafter was born in sin as the Bible says:

Psalm 51:5

"Behold, I was shaped in iniquity; and in sin did my mother conceive me."

That's why in the gospel according to:

John 3:3

"Jesus answered and said unto him, Verily, verily, I say unto thee, except a man be <u>born again</u>, he cannot see the kingdom of God."

How does God deal with the human race?

After God created man He gave him the rulership over His creation.

Genesis 1:28

"And God blessed them, and God said unto them, be fruitful, and multiple and replenish the earth and subdue it: and have dominion over the fish of the sea, and over the fowl of the air, and over every living thing that moves upon the earth."

God gave them a certain amount of power over the animal family. God also has given man the power of choice.

Joshua 24:15

"And if it seem evil unto you to serve the Lord, choose you this day whom ye will serve; whether the gods which you fathers served that were on the other side of the flood, or the gods of the Amorites, in whose land ye dwell: but as for me and my house, we will serve the Lord."

He wants us to choose the good over the evil. He wants us to choose his way and not our own way. He wants us to choose to Love and not Hate.

God is a Loving and just God, yet he doesn't bombard our lives for us to choose his way. He says:

Romans 12:17

"Recompense to no man evil for evil. Provide things honest I the sight of all men."

Romans 12:21

"Be not overcome of evil but overcome evil with good."

On a broad spectrum, God deals with nations:

Genesis 18:18

"Seeing that Abraham shall surely become a great and mighty nation, and all the <u>nations</u> of the earth shall be blessed in him?"

In the New Testament God tells us what he says about nations:

Acts 17:26

"And hath made of one blood all nations of men for to dwell on all the face of the earth, and hath determined the times before appointed, and the bounds of their habitation;"

God deals with man individually. He tells us in (Romans 12:3)

"To every man that is among you, not to think of himself more highly than he ought to think;"

This is because we need to think like God thinks since He is the one who made us and not us ourselves.

He said again in

Ecclesiastes 3:20

"All go unto one place; all are of the dust, and all turn to dust again."

Ecclesiastes 12:7

"Then shall the dust return to the earth as it was: and the spirit shall return unto God who gave it."

1 Peter 1:24-25

"For All flesh is as grass, and all the glory of man as the flower of grass. The grass withers, and the flower thereof falls away;"

God's word is not going to change, for the word of the Lord endures <u>forever</u>.

God made Humans different. Each of us is different. We're designed by God to be different. No one is superior or better than the other. We all have the same fate.

We all have hearts and kidneys and livers to keep us alive and blood that runs through our veins. We all will live on the earth for a time and then we leave. Smart people, all people will die someday, rich or poor all will go.

All our inside is the same and that's what God deals with the nations and the people in the nations.

Paul teaches us the following:

1 Corinthians 4:6.

"And these things, brethren, I have in a figure transferred to myself and to <u>Apollos</u> for <u>your</u> sakes; that ye might learn in us not to think of <u>men above</u> that <u>which</u> is <u>written</u>, that no <u>one</u> of <u>you be puffed up for one against another</u>."

40

Oh!If we humans could just come to that meeting of the minds to know that God the creator, the maker, the manufacturer of humans has made us different, all individuals are different but not better than others. Many may have more possessions, education, money power, and health. No matter what, no one in the earth is better than you. We have all the same fate, pull our skin back we would all be red and have red blood.

God deals with the <u>mind</u> of man.

The mind is the reasoning facility of an individual: Memory; intention

It is where perception in (Luke 9:46-48) Jesus knew what was on their minds:

Luke 9:46-48

"Then there arose a reasoning among them, which of them should be greatest."

v47

"And Jesus, perceiving the thought of their heart, took a child, and set him by him,"

v48

"and said unto them, Whosoever shall receive this child in my name receiveth me: and whosoever shall receive me receiveth him that sent me: for he that I least among you all, the same shall be great."

In my lifetime, when I was a young Christian they used to say, if God caused you to be great in Him, always stay small in your own eyes. Another example concerning our mind is what the Bible tells us in

41

Isaiah 26:3

"Thou wilt keep him in perfect peace, whose mind is stayed on thee: because he trusts in thee."

No one can know what's on your mind but God.

Psalm 139:1-4

"O Lord, thou hast searched me, and known me."

v2:

"Thou know my down sitting and mine uprising, thou understands my thought afar off."

God always knows what's on our minds. He knows our thoughts before we think them.

v3

"Thou compass my path and my lying down, and art acquainted with all my ways."

v4

"for there is not a word in my tongue, but, lo, O Lord, thou knowest it altogether."

In this entire Psalm 139 God is telling us that He knows what is on the mind of everyone, He knows thoughts before we think. He knows what we are going to think and that's with every human being.

He knows whether there is Love or Hate, bias or evil. No one can deceive God.

God tells the Christian, Let not mind be in you which was in Christ Jesus. (Philippians 2:5) Christ's mind is his word. In the word of God, it will tell us how to live on earth and it will tell us how to treat Him and how to treat one another as well.

Paul has written to us in the book (Romans 12:2) He says:

v2

"and be not conformed to this world: but be ye transformed by the renewing of your <u>mind</u>, that ye may prove what is that good, and <u>acceptable</u>, and perfect, will of God."

This scripture clearly tells us that we can't think like the world thinks. We must renew our minds and think like God thinks and say what god has said in his word. That's why we must read the Bible and study the word, so we can know what the word says and do it.

Know what God has said on any subject.

How does God look at man?

God looks at the <u>Soul</u>, the Body, the Heart, the Mind, the Thoughts, and the Spirit. God's thoughts are the very opposite of ours.

Isaiah 55:8-9

For my thoughts are not your thoughts, neither are your ways my ways, says the Lord.

v9

For as the heavens are higher than the earth, so are my ways, and my thoughts than your thoughts.

God looks at the <u>soul</u> God said in:

43

Ezekiel 18:4.

Behold, all <u>souls</u> are mine; as the soul of the father, so also the soul of the son is mine: the <u>soul</u> that sins, it shall die.

One can't see the <u>soul</u> only God sees the soul that's why only God can judge anyone.

Matthew 7:1.

"Judge not, that ye be not judged."

2 Timothy 4:8.

"The Lord is the righteous judge."

Hebrews 12:2.

"God is the judge of all."

The Body

<u>The body</u> is to be kept pure for the Lord.

Romans 12:1

"I beseech you therefore, brethren, by the mercies of God, that ye present your bodies a living sacrifice, holy, acceptable unto God, which is your reasonable service."

For the Christians, the body is the temple of the Holy Ghost.

1 Corinthians 6:19-20

"What? Know ye not that your <u>body</u> is the temple of the Holy Ghost which is in you, which ye have <u>of God, and you are not your own?</u>"

v20

44

"For ye are bought with a price: therefore glorify God in your body, and in your spirit, which are God's."

The Heart:

1 Samuel 16:7

"But the Lord said unto Samuel, look not on his countenance or on the height of his stature; because I have refused him: for the Lord sees not as man sees; for man looks on the outward appearance, but the <u>Lord</u> looks on the <u>heart</u>."

Psalm 44:21.

"Shall not God search this out? For he know the <u>secrets</u> of <u>the heart</u>."

Jeremiah 17:9.

"The heart is deceitful above all things, and desperately wicked: who can know it? (no-one but God)"

Psalm 139:23

"Search me, O God, and know my <u>heart</u>: try me, and know my <u>thoughts</u>:"

We can ask God to search our <u>hearts</u> because God and God alone can know what's in the <u>heart</u>.

<u>The Mind</u>

God tells the Christians to let this <u>mind</u> be in you which was also in Christ Jesus.

If the Non-Christians don't have the Holy Spirit of Christ they can't have the <u>mind</u> of Christ. They can only have a carnal <u>mind</u>.

Romans 8:6-9

"For to be <u>carnally minded</u> is <u>death</u>; but to be <u>spiritually minded</u> is life and peace."

v7

"Because the carnal <u>mind</u> is enmity against God: for it is not subject to the law of God, neither indeed can be."

v8

"So, then they that are in the flesh cannot please God."

v9

"But ye are not in the <u>flesh</u>, but in the <u>Spirit</u>, if so be that the Spirit of God dwell in you. Now if any man have not the <u>Spirit</u> of Christ, he is none of his."

The Thoughts of God toward Solomon the son of David:

1 Chronicles 28:9

"And thou Solomon my son, know thou the God of thy father, and serve him with a perfect <u>heart</u> and with a willing <u>mind</u>: for the Lord searches all <u>hearts</u>, and <u>understands all</u> the imaginations of the <u>thoughts</u>;"

This scripture lets us know that God searches the <u>heart, mind,</u> and <u>thoughts of man</u>. None of these are part of your outward appearance. The heart, the thoughts, the mind, and the soul are all part of that invisible fabric of man's makeup.

All humans: the outward appearance is fleeting every day:

Paul talks about the Christians in:

2 Corinthians 4:16

> *"For which cause we faint not; but though our <u>outward</u> man <u>perish</u>, yet the <u>inward</u> man is renewed day by day."*

As we see according to the <u>Word</u> of <u>God</u> the <u>inward</u> man is more important to <u>God</u> than the <u>outward</u> man.

The Spirit: God is concerned about everyone having His <u>Spirit</u>. Our own human <u>spirit</u> doesn't profit anything.

John 6:63

> *"It is the spirit that quickens; the flesh profits nothing:"*

James2:26

> *"For as the body without the spirit is dead, so faith without works is dead also."*

This is saying when one doesn't have the spirit of Christ they are spiritually dead and they are not a Christian. The body is not dead, but the spirit is alive.

Romans 8:9b.

> *"Now if any man has not the Spirit of Christ, he is none of his."*

God tells Christians to walk in the Spirit. That is a reference to His Holy Spirit. If we would live by the Spirit of God we would not fulfill the lust of the flesh.

So, now we see souls, minds, hearts, thoughts, spirits, and our bodies are what God is most concerned about.

There is no Scripture that addresses our outward appearance.

Our shape, size, height, eyes, ears, noses, mouth, skin color, how we talk, and how we walk.

These are all less important to God than they are to us.

God judges inward for man's sins, not the skin. God has no respect for persons as we do.

We judge and define people by their education, where they live, size, age, skin color, occupation, financial status, race or ethnology, etc.

There are many more things we will use to judge one another.

Don't misunderstand, we need to be educated, we need money and we need to work. God wants us to live a disciplined and temperance life.

What I want to convey in this book is How God Looks at us and judges us in a different way than man. God is always correct. Evil comes from the heart.

Mark 7:14-15

> *"And when he had called all the people unto him, he said unto them, hearken unto me every one of you, and understand;"*

v15

> *"There is nothing from without a man, that entering into him can defile him: but the things which come out of him, those are they that defile the man."*

Mark 7:20-23

> *"And he said that which cometh out of the man, that defiles the man."*

Everything evil that man does comes from the heart.

v21

> *"For from within, out of the heart of men, proceed evil thoughts, adulteries, fornications, murders,"*

v22

> *"thefts, covetousness, wickedness, deceit, lasciviousness, an evil eye, blasphemy, pride, foolishness;"*

v23

> *"All these evil things come from within, and defile the man."*

And that is what God looks at and He judges the inner man. God views humans the way he made them. God is the manufacturer of all people.

Genesis 1:27

> *"So, God created man in his own image, in the image of God created he him: male and female created he them."*

Genesis 1:31

> *"And God saw everything that he had made, and, behold, it was very good. And the evening and the morning were the sixth day. "*

God made everything at first good but because of that one disobedience of the forbidden fruit, all were born in sin. This alludes to the sin of Adam and Eve. But by the obedience of one Jesus Christ, all can be restored back to God.

Romans 5:10

"For if, when we were enemies, we were reconciled to God by the death of his Son, much more being reconciled, we shall be saved by his life."

Romans 5:19

"For as by one man's disobedience many were made sinners, so by the obedience of one shall many be made righteous."

Chapter 6

The Richness of the Human Race

The All-Wise God, All Seeing and All Knowing is Eternal and Our Creator.

You will find in (Genesis 1:27) that God created humans in His own image.

God created humanity for relationships... relationships with each other, with nature, and with God. However human sin separated us from God. Turning what should have been a loving relationship into one filled with hate and disobedience. (Romans 5:10).

Our All-Wise God is also infinite, which refers to limits. God has no limits, being eternal refers to time. God doesn't have a beginning or an end. Before all things were God already existed.

God says in Revelations 1:8,

> *"I am the Alpha and the Omega. Who is and who was, and who is to be the Almighty."*

God is eternal and existed before everything. It also means that God is the Creator, *no one* created God, but all things were created by Him.

God's existence doesn't depend on anything: he is free from obligation, nor does He owe anything to anyone.

This great God, is beyond the Universe, beyond our intelligence, imagination, and our natural understanding. But yet it is he that made us, and we *did not* make ourselves.

Psalm 100:3.

"Know ye that the Lord he is God: it is he that hath made us, and not we ourselves, we are his people, and the sheep of his pasture."

According to this scripture:

We are the product of God's making, God didn't make any junk.

Psalm 139:14,17-18

"I will praise thee: for I am fearfully and wonderfully made: Marvelous are thy works; and that my soul know right well."

That scripture lets us know how carefully and wonderfully he made humans. The heart that beats, the blood that flows through our veins, and the kidney all speak to the wonder of God and the workmanship we are as humans. We talk, we walk, we eat, we sleep, we feel emotion; we cry when we are sad or angry and we laugh when we are happy.

v17

"How precious also are thy thoughts unto me, O God!"

v18

"If I should count them, they are more in number than the sand: When I awake, I am still with thee."

Meaning that God's thoughts are always on us; no one can count the sand, so none can count how much God thinks of us.

He also knows the hair on our head, and how many hairs we have. We have no way of counting them, but God knows <u>how many there are</u>.

So, we are uniquely and richly made. All human beings are richly and uniquely made on the inside. Many times, people will hate others and they will judge others before they get to know the real person. One's outside skin is not the real person. Your heart, mind, and soul are your true character.

The meaning of character is the combination of many things it may be emotional, intellectual, and moral qualities that distinguish an individual.

In some cases, it is conduct, ability, or moral excellence. It is one's goodness, fairness, and strength that is the foundation of a person of great character.

Too many people judge others by trivial things. I would say they are looking at the exterior rather than the interior. It is because we humans can't see the inside of a person.

So, we will judge a person's status, education, race, the color of their skin, the place they live and so on. Most times, these things will divide us.

That's why we need God's word for guidance, our direction, our balance, our counsel, and our divine information as our influence. The word of God says:

Psalm 100:3.

"Know ye that the Lord he is God: it is he that hath made us, and not we ourselves; we are his people, and the sheep of his pasture."

Any object, machinery, vehicle, or anything else is made by a manufacturer. In the case of human life, God Himself is the Maker, the Creator, and the Manufacturer.

So, if we have an object or machine that's not working, correctly we would get out the owner's manual to see how to fix it. At times we can't fix it. So, we will need to send it back to the manufacturer, the one who made it to repair it.

In the case of all human life, God surely knows how to fix, repair, correct, and guide us. He knows how to give us information and counsel of our Creator. We can't go wrong if we obey His word.

God has all the answers to life and we can be and do all that he wants us to do and be.

If we follow His word, we will all have the option to be and do what we can do in this life. According to the Bible:

Ecclesiastes 9:11

"I returned, and saw under the sun, that the race is not to the swift, nor the battle to the strong, neither yet bread to the wise, nor yet riches to men of understanding, nor yet favor to men of skill; but time and chance happens to them all."

Chapter 7

What Did God Mean When He Said *Unequally Yoked?*

God is a Holy God, if one would connect with God, they must be Holy.

Leviticus 11:45

"For I am the Lord that brought you up out of the land of Egypt, to be your God: ye <u>shall therefore be holy, for I am holy</u>. "

God has a way in which he wants his people to live. He demands his people to live Holy live, He said it in the Old Testament and still requires for his people to live Holy <u>in the New Testament</u>.

King Solomon loved many strange women. When God said strange women, he meant women that were not serving the same God: God warned Solomon not to marry those women, because he told Solomon that they would take him away from the real true and living God.

Solomon was warned but he didn't obey, those women were worshipping false gods. So, that's what God means when he says in:

2 Corinthians 6:14

"<u>Be ye not unequally</u> yoked together with unbelievers: for what fellowship hath righteousness with unrighteousness? And what communion hath light with darkness?"

When couples marry, one believes one thing, and the other believes another or doesn't believe at all. They are both not going the same way.

Sometimes, that can cause confusion when couples don't believe the same way. I will share a personal experience with you. Many years ago, I believed in the Bible and would attend church, and my husband would go to the night club and drink heavily and come home and want to fight, so it was very hard to live with him and the children would be very upset. So, that was not a very happy home. He would use profanity that was not good for the family.

That's what God means when he says that don't be unequally yoked together with unbelievers t save you from much <u>chaos</u> and <u>heartache</u>. I am sure it will work much better when we work together, pray together, and work at obeying God's word in the Bible.

When you marry someone who doesn't believe in the Bible, when they believe in doing what they want to do <u>it makes it hard</u>. When God says unequally yoked it means spiritually.

1 Corinthians 7:39

> *"The wife is bound by the law as long as her husband lives; but if her husband be dead, she is at liberty to be married <u>to whom she will; only in the Lord</u>."*

What this scripture means is you are not bound to who you marry, it's not <u>talking</u> about <u>skin color</u>, <u>old</u>, or <u>young</u>, <u>tall</u> or <u>short</u>, <u>rich</u> or <u>poor</u>. (only in the Lord) a person who <u>serves God</u>, <u>a Christian.</u>

God does not deal with one's outward person. God deals with the heart, soul, mind, and spirit, the inside only God knows. He says he knows your thoughts are far off. Even before you think he knows what you are going to think.

56

Chapter 8

Man Must Turn To God!

This is on accurate study on Race according to the Holy Bible. The first book of the Bible is the Book of Genesis, the beginning of creations.

The heaven and the earth, happen by God speaking to what he wants. There is no beginning with God and there is no ending with God:

Psalm 90:2

"Before the mountains were brought forth or ever thou had formed the earth and the world, even from everlasting to everlasting thou art God."

God is an all-seeing God:

Proverbs 15:3

"The eyes of the Lord are in every place, beholding the evil and the good."

God is all-knowing and all-seeing:

Psalm 139:6

"Such knowledge is too wonderful for me; it is high, I cannot attain unto it."

v7

"Whither shall I go from thy spirit? Or whither shall I flee from thy presence?"

v8

"If I ascend up into heaven, thou art there: if I make my bed in hell, behold, thou art there."

v9

"If I take the wings of the morning and dwell in the uttermost parts of the sea;"

v10

"Even there shall thy hand lead me, and thy right hand shall hold me."

v11

"If I say surely the darkness shall cover me; even the night shall be light about me."

v12

"Yea, the darkness hide not from thee; But the night shins as the day: The darkness and the light are both alike to thee."

v13

"For thou hast possessed my reins: Thou hast covered me in my mother's womb."

v14

"I will praise thee; for I am fearfully and wonderfully made: Marvelous are thy works; and that my soul knows right well."

v15

"My substance was not hid from thee, when I was made in secret, and curiously wrought in the lowest parts of the earth."

v16

"Your eyes did see my substance yet being unperfect; and in the book all my members were written, which in continuance were fashioned, when as yet there was none of them."

My thoughts: O Lord you saw all people before they were born because you are the maker and creator of all human life.

You know all the thoughts of all human people. The Lord knows the thoughts before they even get to the mind. He says He knows the thoughts when they are far off. He is acquainted with all our ways.

He knows what every human being is capable of and what we are not capable of: He knows everything there is to know about every human being that's on the earth and that has already left the earth.

I will sum up this section of this chapter by saying Man Must Turn to God and receive his spirit.

He offers his spirit and his power and resources, which will give us the ability to Love our neighbor and give us the ability to Love our enemy.

We will need it in the world we live in today. All the trouble, confusion, and hate are at an all-time high. God's spirit is Love and not hate. God's spirit is good and not evil. God is such a wonder because he allows man to make his own choice when it comes to him.

He doesn't force anyone to choose him. He says whosoever will let them come to him. God Loves people so much that he gave his life through Jesus Christ. If one doesn't choose him, he still blesses them. He doesn't love the sin, but He love the person.

People do evil things, hate, kill, all kinds of evil, God hates the evil, not the individual. Sin always must be punished. You may get away by man's law here on earth, but not with God's law.

Chapter 9

The Final Judgment of Man

Ecclesiastes 8:5-6

> *"Whoso keeps the commandment shall feel no evil thing: and a
> wise man's <u>heart discerns both time and judgment</u>."*

Those who obey him will not be punished. The wise man will find
a time and a way to do what he says.

v6

> *"Because to every purpose there is time and <u>judgment</u>, therefore
> the misery of man is great upon him."*

We all have the same fate in this life. No matter what, race you are
God has all the power.

No one can hold back his or her spirit from being departed: no one
has the power to prevent his day of death.

I have thought deeply about all that goes on here in the world,
where people have the power to injure each other.

But I am comforted to know what the Bible says:

Romans 14:10

> *"But why dost thou judge thy brother? or why dost thou set at
> nought thy brother? for we shall all stand before the <u>judgment seat</u>
> of Christ."*

v11

"For it is written, as I live, says the Lord, every knee shall bow to me, and every tongue shall confess to God.

That's all people, no matter what color you are on the outside.

Your skin doesn't sin, your skin doesn't hate, your skin doesn't kill, your skin doesn't Love: everything happens from the heart.

No one can change until their heart changes and only God can change the heart.

Romans 2:11

"For there is no respect of persons with God.

James 2:9

"But if ye have respect of persons ye commit sin.

Many of us have respect of persons with respect to education, money, wealth, where we live, politics, race, etc.

But God said in His word He will execute judgement:

Jude 1:15

"To execute judgment upon all, and to convince all that are ungodly among them of all their ungodly deeds which they have ungodly committed, and of all their hard speeches which ungodly sinners have spoken against him."

These are the final Judgment of Man that God has said in His word.

Many have gotten away with murder on this earth, but not with God. Many got away because of bias and other reasons.

Revelations 21:7-8

"He that overcomes shall inherit all things, and I will be his God, and he shall be my son."

v8

"But the fearful, and unbelieving, and the abominable, and murderers, and whoremongers, and sorcerers, and idolaters, and all liars, shall have their part in the lake which burns with fire and brimstone: which is the second death.

Chapter 10

God's Word has the Final, Ultimate Answer

If we as Humans believe and know what the word of God says about human life, God does not think like man.

Isaiah 55:8-9

"For my thoughts are not your thoughts, neither are your ways my ways, says the Lord."

v9

"For as the heavens are higher than the earth, so are my ways higher than your ways, and my thoughts than your thoughts."

These scriptures let us know that God doesn't think like us.

Genesis 1:27:

"So God created mankind in his own image, in the image of God he created them; male and female he created them."

What that scripture is saying is if you are living, she is your mother, generations, and generations back to the beginning of human life.

According to this word, Adam and Eve were the first human parents.

The reaffirmation that God made us and He made us good is shown in Genesis 1:31:

"And God saw everything that he had made, and, behold, it was very good."

It all started with Adam and Eve our human parents and because of Adam and Eve, we are all born in sin.

So, whether you are white, black, Asian, Jew, or gentiles, we were made from the dust. From we come and to dust we go back.

We had nothing to do with what race we were born: and death is not in our hands either.

God said that we all must die someday and we all must be judged when we come before our creator and maker.

Hebrews: 9:27

"And as it is appointed unto men once to die, but after this the judgment:"

God loves everyone that he has made. He doesn't love sin. To have respect of a person is a sin among all the other sins that are named in the Bible.

James 2:9.

"But if ye have respect to persons, ye commit sin, and are convinced of the law as transgressors."

God let us know in:

John 3:16

"For God so loved the world, that he gave his only begotten Son,"

He also lets us know all belong to him in:

Ezekiel 18:4

> *"Behold, all souls are mine; as the soul of the father, so also the soul of the son is mine: the soul that sins, it shall die."*

White, black, Asian, Jews, or Gentiles. When God says die, he means an eternal death. Because of that everyone must seek God for the purpose that you came into the world.

Do remember; that it's not what you do for yourself that will last on the judgment day but only what you do for Christ. Everyone has a purpose for being in the earth. We must find out what that is and get busy doing it. We are all on our way to our eternal home.

The first thing God wants us to do is to obey the Bible. God tells us:

John 3:3-6

> *"Jesus answered and said unto him, Verily, verily, I say unto thee, Except a man be born again, he cannot see the kingdom of God."*

v4

> *"Nicodemus says unto him, How can a man be born when he is old? Can he enter the second time into his mother's womb, and be born?"*

v5

> *"Jesus answered, Verily, verily, I say unto thee, Except a man be born of water and of the Spirit, he cannot enter into the kingdom of God."*

v6

"That which is born of the flesh is flesh; and that which is born of the Spirit is spirit."

When you were born from your mother's womb, all you had was a natural life.

Jesus said be born again he means to be born of the Spirit and that Spirit is the Spirit of Jesus.

The Book of (Romans 8:9) says if any man has not the Spirit of Christ, he is none of his. So, if one is none of his we can't go home with him.

Back in the book of (Genesis) when Adam and Eve sin, it caused all of us to be born in sin.

Romans 5:19

"For as by one man's disobedience many were made sinners, so by the obedience of one shall many be made righteous."

So that's why we must be born again because of the sin of Adam.

You might have been born a good person but that's not enough because the Bible says:

Isaiah 64:6

"But we are all as an unclean thing, and all <u>our righteousness</u> are <u>as filthy rags</u>; and we all do fade as a leaf; and our iniquities, like the wind, have taken us away."

2 Corinthians 5:21

"For He has made him to be sin for us, who knew no sin; that we might be made the righteousness of God in him (Jesus)."

So, God has let us know through the scriptures; that we can only be righteous through Jesus Christ. We must be born of His Spirit; according to the scriptures.

I must tell you how you must be born again according to the scriptures.

Acts 2:38

"Then Peter said unto them, Repent, and be baptized every one of you in the name of Jesus Christ of the remission of sins, and ye shall receive the gift of the Holy Ghost."

After you receive the Holy Ghost according to the scripture (2:38) then according to (Acts 1:8) you will have the power to live Holy and Righteous and God will be pleased with your life as you continue to live according to the Word of God. If we could only think like God thinks and that is according to his word.

God's word in the Bible is how God thinks. His word is how God defines all humans.

When God deals with man, he deals with the inside of man not the outside. He deals with one heart, mind, spirit, soul, body, thoughts, and life.

God doesn't deal with what color of your face, or the size your nose, or the shape of your lips and eye lashes. It doesn't matter to Him how tall or short you are, where you live, what name you have, who's your parents, what education you have, how much money you have or how less you have.

God said in (Psalm 139:14) that we are fearfully and wonderfully made.

Fearfully means we are carefully made every part of us was made for a purpose even the hair in our ear and the hair in our nose.

So, if we think of one person as better than the other or one race is better, we sin because that's what His word says.

James 2:9a

"but if ye have respect to persons, ye commit sin."

The word says we sin, God can't sin against himself. So, we know God doesn't think like that. We need to rethink how we think about people when it comes to race. There is the good, bad, and the ugly in ALL races, or better yet, in ALL ethnicities of people.

God Loves all people that He created, but he hates sin. He Loves the sinner and hates the sin; that's how we are to think. If we don't think like God then we will have respect of persons and will be guilty of sin. We need to ask God to help us not to do that. Remember God loves everyone so nothing gives you the right to hate people. You can hate the evil but not the person. If you hate anyone just pray until that hate is gone.

Chapter 11

The Final Pages

There are Biblical examples of people in the Bible who were racist.

Exodus 2:16-22

> *"Now the priest of Midian had seven daughters: and they came and drew water, and filled the troughs to water their father's flock."*

v17

> *"And the shepherds came and drove them away: but Moses stood up and helped them, and watered their flock."*

> *v18*

> *"And when they came to Reuel their father, he said, How is it that ye are come soon to day?"*

v19

> *"And they said, An Egyptian delivered us out of the hand of the shepherds, and also drew water enough for us, and watered the flock."*

v20

> *"And he said unto his daughters, And where is he? Why is it that ye have left the man? call him, that he may eat bread."*

v22

"And she bare him a son, and he called his name Gershom: for he said, I have been a stranger in a strange land."

This is the first racist case in Biblical times.

Numbers 12: 1-16

"And Miriam and Aaron spake against Moses because of the Ethiopian woman whom he had married: for he had married an Ethiopian woman."

v2

"And they said, Hath the Lord indeed spoken only by Moses? Hath he not spoken also by us? And the Lord heard it."

v3

"(Now the man Moses was very meek, above all the men which were upon the face of the earth.)"

v4

"And the Lord spoke suddenly unto Moses, and unto Aaron, and unto Miriam, Come out ye three unto the tabernacle of the congregation. And they three came out."

v

"And the Lord came down in the pillar of the cloud, and stood in the door of the tabernacle, and called Aaron and Miriam: and they both came forth."

v6

"And he said, Hear now my words: If there be a prophet among you, I the Lord will make myself known unto him in a vision, and will speak unto him in a dream."

v7

"My servant Moses is not so who is faithful in all mine house."

v8

"With him will I speak mouth to mouth, even apparently, and not in dark speeches; and the similitude of the Lord shall he behold: wherefore then were ye not afraid to speak against my servant Moses?"

v9

"And the anger of the Lord was kindled against them; and he departed."

v10

"And the cloud departed from off the tabernacle; and, behold Miriam became leprous, white as snow: and Aaron looked upon Miriam, and, behold, she was leprous."

v11

"And Aaron said unto Moses, Alas, my Lord, I beseech thee, lay mot the sin upon us, wherein we have done foolishly, and wherein we have sinned."

v12

"Let her not be as one dead, of whom the flesh is half consumed when he cometh out of his mother's womb."

v13

"And Moses cried unto the Lord, saying, Heal her now, O God, I beseech thee."

v14

"And the Lord said unto Moses, If her father had but spit in her face, should she not be ashamed seven days? Let her be shut out from the camp seven days, and after that let her be received in again."

v15

"And Miriam was shut out from the camp seven days: and the people journeyed not till Miriam was brought in again."

v16

"And afterward the people removed from Hazeroth, and pitched in the wilderness of Paran."

God was not pleased back then, when Moses' sister and brother complained about who Moses married. It was a sin and they were punished with leprosy.

God forgave them, and He healed them. God is not pleased today when his people hate each other. No matter what race of people it is. He made us all, and he loves us all. It is him that made us different skin colors on the outside.

This concludes the 1st edition of this book that I was so very passionate about doing. Many of the scriptures and statements bare repeating over and over because of this critical time in our society that shows so much hate, violence, racial division, and murder. As we see, in all the hatred in the world today God is still speaking in the Bible. He tells us in the scriptures:

Matthew 24:4-13

"And Jesus answered and said unto them, Take heed that no man deceive you."

v5

"For many shall come in my name, saying, I am Christ; and shall deceive many."

v6

"And ye shall hear of <u>wars</u> and <u>rumours</u> of <u>wars</u>: see that ye be not troubled: for all these things must come to pass, but the end is not yet."

v7

For nation shall rise against nation, and kingdom against kingdom: and there shall be famines, and pestilences, and earthquakes, in divers places.

v8

"All these are the beginning of sorrows."

v9

"Then shall they deliver you up to be afflicted, and shall kill you: and ye shall be hated of all nations for my name's sake."

v10

"And then shall many be offended, and shall betray one another, and shall hate one another."

v11

"And many false prophets shall rise, and shall deceive many."

v12

"And because iniquity shall abound, the love of many shall wax cold."

v13

"But he that shall endure unto the end, the same shall be saved."

These scriptures allow us to know what's going on in the world today. There are many others who tell us about what happened in the last days in which we live.

As I have said many times before in this book, God is our Creator, Maker, and the Manufacture of all human life. We understand with our intelligence that when a manufacturer makes a product the maker would understand how that product is supposed to work or function. The Bible tells us in:

Our Creator knows everything about all of His creations. The best way to get along in this world is to follow the guide book which is the Bible.

There are many today who do not want to embrace the Bible:

Mark 12:30-31

"And thou shall love the Lord thy God with all they hear, and with all thy soul, and with all they mind, and with all thy strength: this is the first commandment."

v31

"And the second is like, namely this, Thou shall love thy neighbor as thyself. There is no other commandment which is greater than these."

If we would strive very strongly to love our neighbor as ourselves, the world would be a much different world. The Bible in (Romans

13:8) says we are to owe no man anything but to love them (it's not speaking of money) we owe our fellow man to love them. If we sincerely love our neighbor as ourselves, we will not harm them.

Other Books Written:

1.   When I Found Love I Found You
2.   The Gift of Giving
3.   Relationships
4.   If You Want to go to Heaven this is the Road to Take

I will pause on some of my writing on this first edition on Race Relations. It is such a broad subject, that it would take 2nd, 3rd, and 4th editions to cover such large converse views on this subject; some contrary, some opposite of others, some good, some bad, and some ugly.

I was inspired by <u>God to</u> write about what <u>He says about His own creation</u> according to the Bible, which is certainly God's word.

I will sum up this edition of this book with these final statements, as I have said many times in this book, but it bears repeating because I want my readers to get this message.

We must say what God says, we must try very hard to think like God thinks about people whom He has made. The Bible tells us that all people are made in the image of God.

<u>We were all made from the same material, all races of human beings.</u>

So, what we must understand is that God did not make or create any race better than the other, we are different but none better than the other. The scripture clearly says Eve is the mother of all living, if you are living she is your mother (that is the first woman God made). So, all the generations from generations from generations back to eve. She is the mother and Adam is the first man made from dust.

So, the word of God lets us know that we all have the same fate in life here on earth. We are going to live on earth for a while and then we die that's with all races of people. We all eat and sleep, no one keeps themselves. We must know and believe the Word of God.

2 Corinthians 5:10

"For we must all appear before the judgment seat of Christ: that every one may receive the things done in his body, according to that he hath done, whether it be good or bad."

This scripture lets us know that we all are going to be judged by God on things that we have done on this earth, in our bodies, whether it be good or bad: That's All People.

Romans 2:6

"Who will render to every man according to his deeds: (God)"

v11

"For there is no respect of persons with God."

There were men in the Bible that had respect of persons. Peter in the book of Acts 10th chapter, God told him to go to Cornelius' house and He did not want to, but God allowed him to have a vision. He fell into a trance, God allowed him to see that God receives everyone.

Acts 10:34

"Then Peter opened his mouth, and said, Of a truth I perceive that God is no respecter of persons."

God says in the scripture:

Proverbs 24:23

> *"These things also belong to the wise. It is <u>not good to have</u>*
> *<u>respect of persons in judgment.</u>"*

2 Chronicles 19:7

> *"Wherefore now let the fear of the Lord be upon you; take heed*
> *and do it: for there in no iniquity with the Lord our God, nor*
> *taking of gifts."*

There are many times God has repeated this Word, He wants us to get it.

2 Samuel 14:14b

> *"Neither doth God respect any person:"*

Ephesians 6:9b

> *"Knowing that your Master also is in heaven; neither is there*
> *respect of persons with him."*

Colossians 3:25

> *"But he that doeth wrong shall receive for the wrong which he*
> *hath done: and there is no respect of persons."*

Since we know that God our maker, and creator <u>has no respect of</u> <u>persons</u>, why do we continue to hate people of another race? As stated earlier, hating someone for whatever reason is the spiritual equivalent to killing them. And surely, God is not pleased with His creation hating one another. For He says in James 2:9:

> *"But if ye have respect to persons, ye commit sin, and are*
> *convinced of the law as transgressors."*

A True Story

A friend of mine had the golden opportunity to speak with a married couple, who happened to be people of color. She wanted to hear their views on Racism, Biases, and Prejudices. The couple was over sixty years of age and had contrasting views on the subjects.

The wife who had been saved and filled with the Holy Ghost recounted an incident she had thirty years earlier. While she was sitting on her front porch, she said, the neighbor's four-year-old girl came over from next door where she lived with her parents and two siblings. To her amazement, the little girl asked her a question that stunned her to her core. "Mrs. Jones," she asked, "Did you know that white people are better than black people"?

The question infuriated Mrs. Jones to the point all she could say was, "Mary Beth, it is time for you to go home". Needless to say, the family moved away approximately three months after the incident.

Mr. Jones had gotten up early one morning to go and look for a job. He went to the next town to apply for a factory job that paid more than the job he had been laid off from. Mrs. Jones told the story of how her husband was standing in line with several men who also were of color. There was also in this line a white person who apparently also was seeking employment.

While they all were waiting there, another man who happened also to be caucasian came outside to where the men were standing and announced that all the jobs had been filled. With great disappointment, the men turned and started to walk away. As they were walking away the hiring representative from the factory said to the white individual, "Wait, not you, I want to talk to you." One of the black men said to another, "Did you see that"? "He will talk to the white guy, but not to us".

Some might say, "Yeah, but that was so many years ago". But the question has to be asked, "How much has changed from then to now?" We have had 46 presidents. The 44th President was a black man. With God, there is no respect of persons. If we say that we are in fellowship with God and that this nation was founded on Christian principles then why is there so much respect of persons based on what they look like or don't look like.

According to God's word if we have respect of persons we are sinners and are judged by God's law as being transgressors. If we are going to ever get a handle on this scourge that has plagued this society, we can start by being reminded that God has made of ONE blood all nations to dwell on the face of the earth. We must come to terms with the reality that every man and woman is brother and sister to each other regardless of the myriad of differences in our physical features.

The late Dr. Jack Cottrell, Professor of Theology at Cincinnati Christian University makes the observation:

We are no more permitted to harm a man's spirit than we are his body. The Bible shows that to attack another person verbally or even mentally is a form of murder. Jesus included verbal abuse, including hurling derogatory names and insults toward someone as murder (Matthew 5:21-22).

It is in this light that we must understand the sin of racism. It is a form of murder; an attack on the personhood and humanity of a whole demographic of people.

We must give careful thought and consideration to the words we lob at people or to make ourselves feel more than what we are by viewing others in a light that is less than what God made that person to be.

Summary

There are many undeniable similarities in all the groups of the human family. The Maker and Manufacturer of the human race has designed that whatever happens to one group, happens to another. For instance, death is one of the main things we all have in common regardless of what we see when we look in the mirror.

Job 14:1

"Man that is born of a woman is of a few days and full of trouble".

This is a statement that speaks to literally every man without any exemptions. Even if we would live to be 100 years old (there are many who have) in the larger scheme, when weighed against the longevity of our eternal state after we die, it only amounts to just a few days.

God does not reckon time in the same manner in which man does. A thousand years in God's sight are but as yesterday when it is past; and as a three-hour watch in the night (Psalm 90:4). No one lives forever in this earthly plane. Once we have spent the number of days allotted to each of us we die. It is very important for us not to take God out of our reasoning since it was He who created us.

Because of the broadness of this subject (racism), it is literally impossible to exhaust everything that needs to be said on the matter. This one edition definitely does not suffice to address everything that could be said. It is an ongoing issue that demands more attention and should be debated in peaceful forums, especially here in the United States of America.

When a particular product we have purchased malfunctions, we often go to the manufacturer of that product to resolve the fault. The manufacturer troubleshoots the symptoms and then walks us through the process of what it takes to get the product to work like it was originally designed when it was first manufactured.

In a much larger sense, in order for man to operate or conduct himself in a proper way toward his fellow man and woman it is imperative we consult the Maker of man, God. His word serves as the 'manual' we need to consult to determine whether we are conducting ourselves rightly or wrongly toward someone who does not resemble us, but yet made by the SAME Creator. This is a fact that has been reiterated many times over in this book.

My hope for everyone who reads is that they will come to the same conclusion that I have come when examining this sensitive subject through the eyes of God's Holy Word. The blueprint is laid out so clearly for us to follow if we would. *"What Does God Think About Racism"* is the question asked in the title. But an even more curious question that can be asked is: "What do *YOU* think about racism"?

Extended Scriptural References

Proverbs 19:21

> *"There are many devices in a man's heart; nevertheless, the*
> *counsel of the Lord, that shall stand."*

This verse means that people may plan all kinds of things, but the will of the Lord shall stand.

Psalms 100:3

> *"Know ye that the Lord he is God: it is he that made us, and not*
> *we ourselves."*

We are not our own persons.

Acts 17:28

> *"For in him we live, and move, and have our being;"*

No one can move or even live without our maker. God is very serious about anyone who has respect of person because He considers it a sin.

James 2:9

> *"But if ye have respect to persons ye commit sin and are convinced*
> *of the law as transgressors."*

There are many times God repeats that He has no respect of persons and He does not want man to have respect of persons. Please read that in the Bible. Did you notice, He added an 's' to person? He says it again in

2 Chronicles 19:7

"Wherefore now let the fear of the Lord be upon you; take heed and do it; for there is no iniquity with the Lord our God, nor respect of persons nor taking of gifts."

2 Samuel 14:14

"For we must needs die, and are as water spilt on the ground, which cannot be gathered up again; neither doth God respect any person: yet doth he devise means, that his banished be not expelled from him."

Proverbs 24:23

"These things also belong to the wise. It is not good to have respect of persons in judgment."

Proverbs 28:21 repeats

"To have respect of persons is not good:"

It is we human beings that have respect of persons. We judge people if they are rich or educated or where they live and even the color of their skin.

Galatians 6:10

"As we have therefore opportunity, let us do good unto all men, especially unto them who are of the household of faith."

Jeremiah 31:3.

"The LORD hath appeared of old unto me, saying, Yea, I have loved thee with an everlasting love: therefore with loving kindness have I drawn thee."

God will eventually take his people away as it is written in the Bible and that's the word of God.

1 Thessalonians 4: 15,16-17

"For this we say unto you by the word of the Lord, that we which are alive and remain unto the coming of the Lord shall not prevent them which are asleep."

v16

"For the Lord himself shall descend from heaven with a shout, with the voice of the archangel, and with the trump of God: and the dead in Christ shall rise first:"

v17

"then we which are alive and remain shall be caught up together with them in the clouds, to meet the Lord in the air: and so shall we ever be with the Lord."

God shall take his church away. Then He will go back and save Israel. Do you want to be in the number?

That will be people of all nations and individuals from all the Human Races. We are commanded to love one another. God has given us a command to Love one another. All through the Bible; the Lord has given us that command to Love one another.

God has repeated himself over and over again, (God means what He says) if we could just obey that one command. We would have less crime if any. The four-letter word Love is stronger than Hate.

1 John 3:11

"For this is the message that ye heard from the beginning, that we should Love one another."

1 John 3:23

87

"And this is his <u>commandment</u> that we should believe on the name of his son <u>Jesus Christ</u>, and <u>Love one another</u>, as he gave us his <u>commandment</u>."

1 John 4: 7-12

"Beloved, let us <u>Love one another</u>: for <u>Love</u> is of God; and every one that <u>Love</u> is born of God, and knows God."

v8

"He that <u>Love</u> no know not God; for God is <u>Love</u>."

v9

"In this was manifested the <u>Love</u> of God toward us, because that God sent his only begotten Son into the world, that we might live through him."

v10

"Herein is <u>Love</u>, not that we <u>Loved</u> God, but that he <u>Loved</u> us, and sent his Son to be the propitiation for our sins."

v11

"Beloved, if God so <u>Loved</u> us, we ought also to <u>Love one another</u>."

v12

"No man hath seen God at any time. If we <u>Love one another</u>, God dwells in us, and his <u>Love</u> is perfected in us."

1 John 4:16

"And we have known and believed the <u>Love</u> that God hath to us. God is <u>Love</u>; and he that dwells in <u>Love</u> dwells in God, and God in him."

1 John 4:20-21

"If a man say, I Love God, and hates his brother, he is a liar: for the that love not his brother whom he hath seen, how can he Love God whom he hath not seen?"

v21:

"And this commandment have we from him, that he who Loves God Love his brother also."

1 Thessalonians 3:12

"And the Lord make you to increase and abound in Love one toward another, and toward all men, even as we do toward you:"

1 Thessalonians 4:9

"But as touching brotherly Love ye need not that I write unto you: for ye yourselves are taught of God to Love one another."

Romans 12:10

"Be kindly affectionate one to another with brotherly Love; in honor preferring one another;"

Romans 13:10

"Love works no ill to his neighbor: therefore Love is the fulfilling of the law. Love does not work ill to his neighbor. If you Love like God told us to Love(we won't harm them), we won't kill them."

We not only should love everyone, God tells us to but also love our enemies.

Matthew 5:44

"But I say unto you, Love your enemies,"

Man must turn to God.

Psalm 121:2...

"My help cometh from the Lord, which made heaven and earth. "

This psalmist lets us know where our help comes from (the Lord). We all need help outside of ourselves. We can't always help ourselves because in Him we live, and move, and have our being; (Acts 17:28a).

We always need God's help whether we admit it or not. Jesus says in John 15:5c:

"for without me ye can do nothing."

Since all our help comes from the Lord we can do nothing without him. Man must <u>turn</u> to God for help. If we keep coming to God and <u>true</u> to him with all our hearts, he will not <u>turn</u> us away.

Joel 2:12

"Therefore also now, says the Lord, <u>Turn</u> ye even to me with all your heart."

You see Jesus wants us to <u>turn</u> to Him with <u>all</u> our heart, not half-hearted.

Again He says in Lamentations 3:40

"Let us search and try our ways, and <u>Turn</u> again to the Lord."

We all should repent and <u>turn</u> to God. (He will be pleased). All belongs to Him.

Timothy 6:7

"For we brought nothing into this world, and it is certain we can carry nothing out."

Romans 12:16

"Be of the same mind one toward another. Mind not high things, but condescend to men of low estate. Be not wise in your own conceits."

Romans 12:18

"If it be possible, as much as lies in you, live peaceably with all men."

James 4:11-12

"Speak no evil one of another, brethren. He that speaks evil of his brother, and judges his brother, speaks evil of the law, and judges the law: but if thou judge the law, thou are not a doer of the law, but a judge."

v12

"There is one lawgiver, who is able to save and to destroy: who are thou that judges another?"

Romans 12:10

"Be <u>Kindly Affectionate one</u> to another with brotherly love; in honor <u>preferring one</u> another;"

Philippians 2:3

"Let nothing be done through strife or vainglory; but in lowliness of mind let each esteem other better than themselves."

Ephesians 5:2

"Submitting yourselves one to another in the fear of God."

Ephesians 4:32

"And be ye kind one to another, tenderhearted, forgiving one another, even as God for Christ's sake hath forgiven you."

Author's Biography

Evangelist Louise Hamilton has been an active member of the Bethesda Temple Church of the Apostolic Faith, Inc. for 47 years under the leadership of the late Bishop James A. Johnson.

Evangelist Hamilton has been called by God, to work, to teach and preach the word of God. She has worked as a Sunday School Teacher and Outreach Director. She has also taught in Children and nursing homes. She has worked in the St. Louis Public School District as a teacher's aide. Evangelist Hamilton also served as Personal Aide to the Honorable Edith Spink, Mayor of Ladue between the years of 1987-2002.

She has worked both high and lows of serving others, she defines herself as just a servant, which has given her the experience to help and interact with people.

Evangelist Hamilton attended the Harris Stowe Teacher's College, Layer College Aenon Bible College, and the Bethesda Bible Institute receiving certificates. In 1997 she was ordained in the Midwestern District Council. Evangelist Hamilton still resides in St. Louis, Missouri, and is presently a faithful member of the Bethesda Temple Church of the Apostolic Faith, now Pastored by Suffragan Bishop Julian R. Johnson.

Other Books by Evangelist Louise Hamilton

1. The Gift of Giving
2. Do You Want to Go to Heaven?
3. This is the Road to Take
4. When I Found Love I Found You
5. The Love of God
6. The Commendable Work of Various Ladies

Made in the USA
Monee, IL
10 February 2024